TO LIVE
LIKE A TREE
ALONE AND FREE
LIKE A FOREST
IN BROTHERHOOD

Organized by

Founded in 1987, **American Turkish Association of North Carolina (ATA-NC)** is a non-profit, member supported organization dedicated to promoting awareness of Turkish culture and sharing Turkish heritage throughout the state of North Carolina.

Sponsored By

 The 2015 Nazim Hikmet Poetry Festival has been made possible by a major grant from the Turkish Cultural Foundation (www.turkishculturalfoundation.org)

Hosted and Sponsored By

| TOWN OfCARY | Parks, Recreation & Cultural Resources | www.townofcary.org |

Support Also Provided By

 www.sistercitiesofcary.org

Organizing Committee
Buket Aydemir, Pelin Balı, Erdağ Göknar, Richard Krawiec, Mehmet C. Öztürk, Birgül Tuzlalı

Cover Design by Pelin Balı
Prepared for Publication by Pelin Balı
Copyright: American Turkish Association of North Carolina

Seventh Annual
Nâzım Hikmet Poetry Festival

April 26, 2015 • Page Walker Arts & History Center • Cary, NC

Table of Contents

Preface — 6

Nâzım Hikmet — 8

Invited Talk — 11
  Anna Akhmatova by Stanislav Shvabrin

Invited Poet - Betty Adcock — 25

Poetry Competition — 29

  Poetry Competition Selection Committee — 30

  Finalists — 33
    Leila Chatti — 35
    Lois Harrod — 39
    Mimi Herman — 47
    Emily Jaeger — 51
    Edison Jennings — 55
    Anne Whitehouse — 59
    Andy Young — 69

  Honorable Mentions — 77
    Jane K. Andrews — 79
    Mary Elizabeth Parker — 85
    Mike Saye — 95

Turkish Poetry Translations — 99
  Behçet Necatigil by Hatice Örün & Jeffrey Kahrs — 100

Artist, Pelin Balı — 105

Preface

The Nâzım Hikmet Poetry Festival brings together poets, scholars and the community in a one-day annual event celebrating poetry and honoring the Turkish poet Nâzım Hikmet. The festival has become a major forum for cultural exchange and a mainstay of the local and global cultural landscape.

The focus of the Seventh Nâzım Hikmet Poetry Festival was the Russian poet, Anna Akhmatova and her poetry. Our invited speaker was Dr. Stanislav Shvabrin, professor of Russian literature at UNC-Chapel Hill. He was joined on stage by his colleague, Dr. Irene Masing-Delic. We are grateful to both of them for their delightful contribution to our festival. Dr. Shvabrin's original article on Anna Akhmatova in this book provides an intimate account of Akhmatova's life, her immense struggles under the Stalin regime and her poetry.

Betty Adcock was the invited poet of this year's festival. Ms. Adcock is the recipient of numerous honors including three Pushcart Prizes, fellowships from the Guggenheim foundation and the National Endowment of Arts. In 2014, she was inducted into the North Carolina Literary Hall of Fame. We would like to express our sincere gratitude to Ms. Adcock for her immense contribution to our festival. Her poem, *Ode on a guinea pig* is included in this book.

We are grateful to Anatoly Larkin for his memorable performance of Russian masters on piano. His music will be remembered as one of the highlights of this year's festival.

Pelin Bali, one of the organizers of our festival created the original watercolor portrait of Anna Akhmatova decorating the front cover of this book. We feel lucky to have such a talent on our team.

This year's poetry competition received over 1000 poems from 337 poets. The submissions came from 39 states and 20 countries. North Carolina poets submitted 26.3% of the poems. 14% of the poems were submitted from other countries. The final selection committee included Joseph Bathanti, Greg Dawes, Erdağ Göknar, Terry Hummer and Jaki Shelton-Green. We are grateful to our judges for their conscientious and magnanimous work. The competition produced seven finalists and three honorable mentions. As it was the case in previous years, the group included both established and rising poets. These poets are now members of the Hikmet family.

This year marks the third year of the Turkish poetry translation project. Hatice Örün and Jeffrey Kahrs contributed to this publications with translations of the Turkish poet, Behçet Necatigil. We are indebted to our translators for their contributions.

The Seventh Nâzım Hikmet Poetry Festival was made possible by a major grant from the Turkish Cultural Foundation (TCF). We would like to extend our gratitude to TCF and especially to Ms. Güler Köknar, executive director of the Foundation, for her continued support. Additional support was provided by Duke University and NC Poetry Society. The Town of Cary (Dept. of Parks, Recreation and Cultural Recourses) provided the venue, the Page Walker Arts & History Center, a poetic setting appropriate to our festival. Special thanks go to Mayor Harold Weinbrecht, Mr. Lyman Collins, and Mrs. Kris Carmichael for their encouragement and support. With the help of this support, we are able to open our doors to the general public free of charge.

Last but not least, we are grateful to all our friends whose volunteer efforts made the festival and this publication possible.

B. Aydemir, P. Balı, E. Göknar, R. Krawiec, M. C. Öztürk & B. Tuzlalı

(1902 - 1963)

Nâzım Hikmet, the foremost modern Turkish poet, was born in 1902 in Selânik. He grew up in Istanbul and was introduced to poetry early, publishing his first poems at the age of 17. He attended the Naval Academy but was discharged due to repeated bouts of pleurisy. Attracted by the Russian revolution and its promise of social justice, he crossed the border and made his way to Moscow and studied Political Science and Economics. He met with poets and other artists of the futurist movement and his style changed from Ottoman literary conventions to free verse.

He returned to Turkey in 1928 and spent five of the next ten years in prison on a variety of trumped-up charges due to his leftist views. During this time, he published nine books that revolutionized Turkish poetry and the Turkish language.

In 1938, he was arrested for supposedly inciting the Turkish armed forces to revolt. He was sentenced to 28 years in prison on the grounds that military cadets were reading his poems. While in prison, he composed some of his greatest poems as well as his epic masterpiece *Human Landscapes from My Country*. He wrote a total of 66,000 lines; according to his letters, 17,000 of those survived.

In 1949, an international committee including Pablo Picasso, Paul Robeson and Jean Paul Sartre was formed in Paris to campaign for his release. In 1950 he was awarded the World Peace Prize, which Pablo Neruda accepted on his behalf. The same year he went on an 18-day hunger strike despite a recent heart attack and was released under the general amnesty of the newly elected government. Following his release, there were repeated attempts to murder him. When he was ordered to do his military service at the age of fifty, he fled the country and was stripped of Turkish citizenship. His citizenship was officially restored by the Turkish government fifty-eight years later on January 5, 2009.

Nâzım Hikmet did not live to see his later poems published in Turkish, although they were translated into more than forty languages during his lifetime. He died of a heart attack in 1963, at the age of sixty-one. During the fifteen years after his death, his eight volume "Collected Poems", plays, novels and letters were gradually published.

Many celebrations of Nazim's 100th birthday took place in 2002: UNESCO named 2002 "The Year of Nâzım Hikmet"; and the American Poetry Review put him on their cover and published a collection of his poems.

Invited Speaker
Stanislav Shvabrin

Anna Akhmatova
(1889 - 1966)

A GUARDIAN OF RUSSIAN MEMORY: ANNA AKHMATOVA'S RHYTHMS AND REASONS

Anna Akhmatova (pseudonym; full actual name Anna Andreyevna Gorenko, 1889-1966), the second most recognizable "alpha" in the ABC of Russian culture, the one that springs to mind immediately after Alexander Pushkin. How does one take the reader past the array of instantly available facts—Wikipedia is but one obvious source—and manages to say something of consequence about someone so well known? This life story has been told and re-told so many times by many a skilled biographer; this woman's face has been drawn, re-drawn, photographed, and reproduced so many times by many a skilled hand. The obvious route would run more or less as follows. One should mention her all-Russian popularity—by the mid-twenties of the century the title of the foremost Russian woman poet, someone who, in her own words, "taught [Russian] women to speak," was indubitably hers. It might be interesting to mention her love affairs (and add that some of those defied the standards of early twentieth-century prudery). Quite important is her refusal to leave her homeland even after it became painfully obvious that Russia was falling prey to a cynical and murderous clique of extremists. One should not forget the decades of torment and terror when Stalin held her only son a hostage (in his spare time the infamous mass-murderer enjoyed inflicting exquisitely inhumane torture on strong-willed individuals). Her late years were spent under Stalin's tamer, if erratic, successor and denouncer Khrushchev; it was then when she was permitted to travel to Italy to receive a literary award and to England to accept an honorary professorship from Oxford, all this happening when in the Soviet Union this elderly woman had to depend on the kindness of friends for room and board… One can spend quite a bit of time and effort recounting these facts and so much of the good and the bad that came in between, yet fail utterly to convince the reader of the reasons why this woman—or her legacy and legend—inspires so much reverence in so many people while continuing to irritate a few of those who still feel tickled by her positively regal manner of treating everyone around her. To put it simply, what is so special about Akhmatova?

    I will attempt to answer this question by focusing on the "what" and the "how" of her verse. I will be using two poems from two stages of her development (a short lyric and a few excerpts from a narrative poem, to be exact) as my examples.

For a taste of Akhmatova's early poetry, let us turn to a fairly early piece that contributes to the tradition of Russia's fascination with the founding father of its modern culture, Alexander Pushkin (1799-1837).

PUSHKIN

A swarthy young boy lolled down pathways
By himself at the edge of the lake.
For a hundred long years we have cherished
The slight rustle his far footsteps make.

The thick, prickly fir-needles pile up
Above the low stumps of each tree...
Here's his three-cornered hat and a dog-eared
Volume of verse by Parny.

1911
(Translated by Vladimir Markov & Merrill Sparks) [1]

The "what" of this poem seems easy enough to grasp. This poem appears to be an exercise in a peculiarly Russian brand of the phenomenon known in the English-speaking world as "bardolatry," which is to say a passionate, country-wide worship of a strong poet ("bard") of Shakespearean stature. A closer look at this same poem reveals that Akhmatova contribution to this tradition is highly unconventional.

The word "worship" introduces into this conversation frankly religious undertones, but if Russians consider Pushkin their culture's demigod (after his death in a duel Pushkin was proclaimed "the Sun of Russian poetry"), Akhmatova chooses to show that deity at the least god-like period of his life, his adolescence. (It is no accident that such and similar moments are frequently omitted from the orthodox versions of sacred texts—the Gospels, for example, carefully avoid talking about their

---

[1] Cited from *Modern Russian Poetry*. An Anthology with Verse Translation Edited and with an Introduction by Vladimir Markov and Merrill Sparks. Indianapolis-New York, The Bobbs-Merrill Company, 1967, p. 257.

protagonist's childhood, teenage years, and young adulthood.) Akhmatova certainly counts herself among those who "cherish" every distant echo of the rustle made by the "swarthy boy's" feet that allegedly still resound across a majestic imperial park in the vicinity of St. Petersburg where Pushkin attended the "Lyceum," an elite boarding school. But what is it that she chooses to focus our attention on next? That boy's reading interests, to be certain. Those who do not know, but decide to find out who Parny was will be surprised that Évariste Parny (French, 1753-1814) was a far cry from a somber epic poet, a paragon and role model for someone who would go on to become an object of national worship and, by inevitable extension, frequent misunderstanding. For Pushkin's contemporaries Parny was synonymous with light and unambiguously erotic poetry, and Pushkin's partiality to that kind of reading suddenly demystifies the cultural icon by showing a human, indeed boyish, aspect of a man whose likenesses is so often cast in bronze.

Akhmatova shows Pushkin, that most Russian of Russians in the eyes of so many, an inalienable part of the tradition of Gallic frivolity, playfulness, and irreverence. If this is an exercise in the portrayal of a national icon, it is decidedly Modernist in its attention to precisely that segment of that icon's significance which the pious and respectable priests of a national cult might like to treat with caution. Akhmatova and her Modernist allies and contemporaries clearly decide to adhere and contribute to the century-old tradition of Pushkin-worship, but in her understated way she makes it plain that if they are going to do so, they are going to do it on their own terms.

To this day more often than not Russian poets continue to express themselves in rhymed verse. The "how" of this short poem—which is to say the purely technical aspect of it rhythmic makeup that comes under the headings of "versification" and/or "poetic prosody"—is every bit as revealing and fascinating as any bit of information it communicates to us directly.

Difficult as it is to appreciate in a translation, this poem is deliberately composed in a prosodic medium that is not exactly Pushkinian. When read out loud, the original meter of this poem does not sound all that similar to the infinitely flexible, but highly regular pulse of Pushkinian iambs. The rhythm of Akhmatova poem not as predictable as they are, here and now it "stumbles," forcing the reader to pause for an instant in places where they may not expect a rhythmic break. If one attempts to scan these lines using the traditional—Pushkinian—matrix, one quickly realizes that the interpretation of this poem's rhythm in terms of the syllabotonic system of Russian classical versification makes little or no sense. Behind the curtain of this poem's meaning, Akhmatova's intimate paean to the spirit of Pushkinian youth and frivolity does away with the highly rational regularity of the Pushkinian poetic meters. The prosody of this poem infuses the Russian tradition with the rhythmic figures that evolved on Russian soil after Pushkin's death under direct influence of Heinrich Heine (1797-1856) and Paul Verlaine (1844-1896) and were perfected by the most influential of Russian Symbolists Alexander Blok (1880-1921).

Implicitly as well as explicitly, Akhmatova marries the tradition of Russian high Classicism and Romanticism forever associated with Pushkin to the experimental unpredictability of Modernism, the prevalent intellectual idiom of her day. She demonstrates that novelty and progress do not necessarily require rupture with the past; she effectively puts herself in the position of a living link between Pushkin and her contemporaries. At the time when Akhmatova's near coevals the Russian Futurists were getting ready to emulate their Italian hero Tommaso Marinetti (1876-1944) by inciting their compatriots "to toss Pushkin from the steamboat of modernity" (something they will do in a 1912 manifesto fittingly entitled "A Slap in the Face of Public Taste"), Akhmatova quietly asserts her own way of moving forward without burning the bridges.

What can be further removed from anything practical, urgent, and palpably material than such ephemeral matters as poetry, poetic rhythms, and the celebration of dead poets? Soon after Akhmatova wrote her "Pushkin," the Russian Empire met its inglorious end in the deserted WWI trenches and the short-lived hope of a free and democratic Russian republic was expertly dashed by a gang of extreme-left dogmatists who believed that they could use Russia as a lever which would set into motion the irreversible mechanisms of a global "anti-capitalist" revolution. Effecting such a change, however, requires more than political will, military hardware, and exceptional luck. Once political power has been seized, people need to be convinced that their habitual way of life, their daily routines, rituals, and traditions are worth little or nothing in comparison with such lofty goals as the establishment of a kingdom of universal equality. Human life and its value need to be reexamined as well, since certain ends must surely justify certain means. It is no coincidence that poets make it difficult for politicians-visionaries to get their job done (none other than Plato famously argued that poets should be banished from the ideal state lest their incite dark, unruly emotions that would upset the ordered life of a perfect commune). First without knowing it, subsequently becoming fully aware of this inescapable fact, Anna Akhmatova proved to be one such difficult person.

Foreigners are often surprised to find out that literature, poetry are assigned such high value in Russia. Literature gets people to high places; literature becomes people's undoing. Russia is universally credited with having an intricate and nuanced literary tradition, for being extremely literate, literary, and verbal. It comes as a discovery to many that parallel to this vocal current of Russian culture runs a current of silence, that Russia constantly vacillates between giving voices to complex notions and refusing to discuss its own past. "There's no point in talking about this, everyone knows what it was all about," argue those who prefer that certain painful, uncomfortable experiences would be left alone, unmentioned and unmentionable. In their midst there are those who truly believe that silence is a virtue and has healing properties as there are those who cleverly use silence as a weapon of mass amnesia. (Today's Russia, Putin's Russia, incidentally, presents a fresh example of how those in the latter category are capable of exploiting the fears of those who belong to the former.) Akhmatova, this one-timer singer of frivolity and intimate universes of residing within ourselves was silenced for the duration of Stalin's reign, but it was she who became one of the most vocal and articulate of Stalin's opponents.

Akhmatova's narrative poem *Requiem* (1935-c.1960-s)— requiem for the countless direct victims of the Great Terror as well as those affected by it indirectly (wives, fathers, sisters, brothers, friends, and, of course, mothers of the "disappeared ones," as was Akhmatova's lot)—is a monument to her ability to emerge from unimaginable sorrow as a keeper, custodian, and guardian of her people's memory.

Akhmatova spoke foreign languages and had friends she could rely on for support all over Western Europe. She could have followed the example of so many of her relatives, friends, and acquaintances and leave Soviet Russia for Western Europe. Improbable, irrational as it may sound, it was her understanding of her duty as a national poet, however, that prevented her from doing what every reasonable person of her intelligence and foresight should have done.

As to her calling, she acknowledged as much in what may well be the most memorable quatrain in the entire canon of Russian poetry:

> from *Requiem*
> The Sentence
>
> No, it wasn't under foreign heavens,
> Nor the shelter of a foreign wing –
> I stood then in my people's presence,
> Where my people, by ill luck, had been.
>
> 1961
> Translation by Sarah Vitali (c) 2016.
> Reproduced by permission

The peculiar art of versemaking is hardly a rational pursuit from the point of view of the average reasonable person: what reasonable woman would busy herself with composing and memorizing elegies mere acquaintance with which would qualify as and act of sedition that in Stalin's USSR was punishable by death? If the example of Akhmatova and that of her early partners in crime is anything to go by, this irrational, suprarational pursuit may well be the only reliable, time-proven defense mechanism available to those who find themselves face to face with premeditated and industrialized mass murder. Yet the significance of this "utilitarian" aspect of her achievement is even more far-reaching. By protecting and asserting her personal dignity through the process of transformation of her personal, individual fear and grief as well as that of her countless fellow victims into haunting verbal imagery that is rendered indelible thanks to her expert use of unforgettable poetic rhythms, Akhmatova was able to counter the dehumanizing effect of silent solitary trauma. The erstwhile singer of heartache and master-painter of St. Petersburg's cityscapes, she became the poet whose words help people deal with the impossible. By virtue of doing so, Akhmatova's *Requiem* qualifies as a purifying, indeed cathartic, event and experience of national proportion. Having asserted her dignity and autonomy from fear, she helped and continues to help countless others to open up to each other, to find the words fitting for designation and discussion of something that must not be permitted to repeat itself. Listening to and reading Akhmatova, therefore, is tantamount to tapping into the contents of the vessel storing that mysterious substance that allows men and women sharing the same geographic space share a traumatic memory. It is to Akhmatova and few others like her that we owe our ability to talk about a trauma the scale of which beggars belief.

Memory as life and amnesia as a form of non-existence are directly named in Akhmatova's *Requiem:*

from *Requiem*
The Sentence

And the stony sentence tumbled leaden
Upon my still-inhaling, beating breast.
It doesn't matter, though, for I was ready.
I'll somehow find a way to make the best.
I've got an awful lot to do today:

I have to put my memory to death,
I have to force my soul to fade away,
I have to teach myself to live again.
And if not… the sultry buzz of summer
Is just as though a carnival had come.
Long ago, I'd seen this moment coming:
This bright day and this emptied home.

1939. Summer
Translation by Sarah Vitali (c) 2016.
Reproduced by permission

Thus Anna Akhmatova can be defined as the poet of traumatic national memory that continues to unite, inspire, and evelate, a person thanks to whom a group of people bound by unspeakable grief finds the words with which to countenance their past and face their future. There is more to her poetry than that, but a recognition of this simple fact is a good starting point for those wishing to make her acquaintance.

***

What follows are two fragments from Georgy Vladimirovich Ivanov's fictionalized memoir book of memoirs *Petersburg Winters* (1952). Ivanov (1894-1958; no relation to Vyacheslav Ivanov who figures in the first fragment reproduced here) most certainly knew Akhmatova personally through her first husband Nikolai Gumilyov (1886-1821)—Ivanov was Gumilyov's follower and member of his circle. Much of what he has to say about Akhmatova is hearsay, but rumors and legends are every bit as powerful in shaping literary reputations as facts. The first fragment concerns Akhmatova's coming out of her husband's shadow on the eve of World War I; the second opens in Paris where Ivanov, a political exile from Soviet Russia, encounters an old acquaintance of his who has managed to escape to Paris from the state-sponsored terror and starvation of the early years of the totalitarian regime that came to rule over Akhmatova's homeland after an internecine civil war of 1917-1922. It would be useful to keep in mind that Akhmatova herself resented Ivanov's memoir for his cavalier attitude toward facts and his desire to impose his vision of other people's lives on the reader. Excerpted from Georgy Ivanov, *Disintegration of the Atom. Petersburg Winters*, translated from the Russian, edited, annotated, and with an introduction by Jerome H. Katsell and Stanislav Shvabrin (Boston, MA, Academic Studies Press, forthcoming 2016).

Georgy Ivanov
from PETERSBURG WINTERS[2]

1911. "The Tower"—Vyacheslav Ivanov's apartment—is hosting one of its literary Wednesdays. All the "crème de la crème" of poetic Petersburg gathers here. Poems are read here in a circle, and the "wise man of Tavrichesky Street," squinting from under his pince-nez and throwing back his golden mane, hands out his verdicts. For the most part they are politely lethal. The cruelty of the verdict is mitigated by only one feature—it is impossible to disagree with its caustic precision. Ivanov's praises, on the contrary,

---

[2] Translated from the Russian by Jerome Katsell and Stanislav Shvabrin. (C) 2016 All right reserved

are extremely meager. The slightest of approvals is a rarity.

Poems are read in a circle. Celebrities and beginners, they all read. The turn comes round to a young lady, thin and dusky.

It is Gumilyov's wife. She "writes too." Well, of course, wives of writers always write, wives of artists busy themselves with paints, wives of musicians play an instrument. It seems that this dark and dusky Anna Andreyevna is not altogether without ability. While still a young lady she wrote:

> And for whom will these pale lips
> Become a fatal potion?
> A Black man behind her, haughty and crude,
> Peers out cunningly...

Sweet, don't you think? It's beyond understanding why Gumilyov becomes so irritated when his wife is spoken about as a poet.

And Gumilyov truly does become irritated. He too looks at her poems as the whim of "a poet's wife." And that whim is not to his taste. When her poems are praised, he smiles derisively. "You like it? I'm so happy. My wife does lovely embroidery as well."

"Anna Andreyevna, will you read us some?"

Condescending smiles spread across the faces of the "genuine ones" present. Gumilyov pulls a dissatisfied grimace and taps a cigarette against his cigarette case.

"I will."

Two spots show on her dusky cheeks. Her eyes look forward bewildered and haughty. Her voice trembles slightly.

"I will."

> My breast turned helplessly cold,
> But my steps were light,
> On my right hand I put
> The glove from my left hand...

An indifferent-amiable smile appears on the faces. Certainly not serious stuff, but pleasing, don't you think? Gumilyov throws away an unfinished cigarette. The two spots stand out even sharper on Akhmatova's cheeks...

What will Vyacheslav Ivanov say? Probably nothing. He will be silent for a bit, then make note of some technical peculiarity. After all, his devastating verdicts are for serious poems of genuine poets. And here we have... Why insult someone for no reason?"

Vyacheslav Ivanov remains silent for a moment. Then he rises, walks up to Akhmatova, kisses her hand.

"Anna Andreyevna, I congratulate you and welcome you. This poem is an event in Russian poetry."

* * *

"La Rotonde." Usual evening hubbub. I look for an empty table. Suddenly, my eyes meet with eyes that once were well known to me (Petersburg, snow, 1913...), gray Russian eyes. It is S., the wife of a famous artist.

"You here! Since when?"

A smile—a distracted "Petersburg" smile: "It's been a month since leaving Russia."

"From Petersburg?"

"From Petersburg."

S. is a friend of Anna Akhmatova. Naturally, one of my first questions is: "How is Akhmatova?"

"Anya? She's still living at the same place on the Fontanka, near the Summer Garden. She doesn't go out much, only to church. She writes, of course. Does she publish? No, she doesn't think about that. How can you publish these days..."

...On the Fontanka. Near the Summer Garden...

1922. Autumn. I'm leaving for abroad the day after tomorrow. I'm going to Akhmatova's to bid my farewell. The Summer Garden already rustles autumnally. Engineers' Castle glows red in the sunset. How deserted it all is! How disturbing! Farewell, Petersburg!

Akhmatova extends her hand to me. "I'm here passing the night away," she says. "Are you leaving for abroad?"

Her delicate profile is outlined in the darkening window. Her shoulders are wrapped in the storied dark shawl with large roses on it:

> O Phaedra, a pseudo-classical shawl
> Slides down from your shoulders...

"Are you leaving for abroad? Convey my regards to Paris."

"And you, Anna Andreyevna, you're not planning to

leave?"

"No. I won't leave Russia."

"But it's getting more difficult to live here."

"Yes, more difficult."

"It may become completely unbearable."

"What can one do?"

"You won't be leaving?"

"I'm not going to leave."

...No, she is not even thinking about publishing—where would she publish now... She doesn't go out much—only to church... Her health? It's becoming worse, true. And life is such that she is forced to do everything for herself. She ought to travel south, to Italy. But where would she get the money? And if she had it...

"She won't be leaving?"

"She won't."

"You know," the gray eyes look at me almost strictly "You know, Anya was walking once along Mokhovoy Street carrying a sack. I think she was carrying some flour. She got tired and stopped to rest. Winter. She was dressed poorly. Some woman or other walked by... She gave Anya a kopeck. 'Take it, for the love of Christ.' Anya hid that kopeck behind her icons. She has been treasuring it ever since..."

Stanislav Shvabrin, a native of Nizhny-Novgorod, Russia, comes to the US via Luxembourg, Belgium and England. Shvabrin holds a Ph.D. in Slavic languages and literatures from UCLA, where he had a singular privilege to study under Michael Henry Heim and work with Vladimir Markov. Shvabrin research focuses on poetics, comparative literary studies, translation studies, and diaspora studies. In addition to his archival research, scholarly and editorial work on Vladimir Nabokov  (*Verses and Versions: Three Centuries of Russian Poetry Selected and Translated by Vladimir Nabokov*, Harcourt Houghton Mifflin, 2008, and *The Original of Laura*, Alfred A. Knopf, 2009), Shvabrin's has written on Georgy Ivanov and Marina Tsvetaeva. Shvabrin has published scholarly essays and archival materials in such periodical outlets as *Comparative Literature*, *Russian Literature* and *Slavic and East European Journal* as well as *Novyi zhurnal* and *Zvezda*. 2015 marks a decade since the appearance of the most representative scholarly edition of Mikhail Kuzmin's poetry, prose, drama and criticism in English, *Selected Writings* (Bucknell University Press). In the US, Shvabrin has taught Russian language, literature, and theater at UCLA, California State University at Northridge and Princeton University. At present he is affiliated with the Department of Germanic and Slavic Languages and Literatures in the University of North Carolina at Chapel Hill.

Invited Poet
Betty Adcock

Betty Adcock

Ode on a Guinea Pig

Borrowing from Kierkegaard,
I love this animal because he is absurd.
A small being lacking ambition,
he carries no heavy affectation of joy
as the dog does, leaping and licking.
He doesn't bargain for comfort like the cat
who sits on your lap only if you stroke her.
He proffers no unpleasant squawks,
no saccharine song. His whistle is sharp
but singular and only for food. It makes
an honest music.

          He does not lie to us:
I am here is the one communication
in his Buddha-sitting, his fat-assed waddle.
The only surprise he offers is the occasional dash,
faster than you'd imagine, to nowhere in particular.
He's no wild thing, nor yet quite tame.

His name is of no interest to him. *Don't
call me*, he could be saying. I would guess his DNA
has nothing of the pig. Or the fox, the deer, the cow.
Perhaps he's related only to philosophers;
or he's a creature of his own imagining,
a plump baby god watching over
an attenuated world.

Betty Adcock

He loves us as he is able, with a deep understanding
of warmth and softness, lettuce leaves and hay.
He appreciates snug openings. Certainly he embodies
the poet's admonition -- not to *mean*
but *to be* (and also Hamlet's, only without
the *or not* part).

There's no creature like him because he has dreamed
no such thing. We should take note of his seemlessness,
bask in that steady gaze, and learn.

> *-for Mollie*

This poem originally appeared in the Cortland Review, an online journal.

Betty Adcock

Betty Adcock grew up in rural East Texas and has lived all her writing life in Raleigh, North Carolina. LSU press has published six collections of her poetry, most recently *Intervale: New and Selected Poems (2002)* which won the Poets' Prize and was a finalist for the Lenore Marshall prize from the Academy of American Poets; and *Slantwise* chosen by LSU press as the Leslie Phillabiaum award volume for 2008. A chapbook, *Widow Poems*, was published by Jacar Press in 2014. Honors include the North Carolina award for literature, the Texas Institute of Letters prize, the Hanes Award from the Southern Fellowship of Writers, three Pushcart Prizes and fellowships in poetry around the state of North Carolina and the National Endowment for the Arts. She held a Guggenheim Fellowship for 2002–2003. Ms. Adcock was Kenan Writer in Residence at Meredith College for twenty years. She has been visiting professor at Duke University, Kalamazoo college in Michigan, Lenoir-Rhyne University, and North Carolina State University. For ten years, she was a faculty member in the low-residency Warren Wilson MFA program for Writers. She's a member off the Texas Institute of Letters and the Fellowship of Southern Writers. In 2014, she was inducted into the North Carolina Literary Hall of Fame. She is completing a seventh full length collection.

Seventh Annual
Nâzım Hikmet Poetry Competition

Poetry Competition Selection Committee
(in alphabetical order)

Joseph Bathanti is former Poet Laureate of North Carolina (2012-14). He is the author of eight books of poetry, including *Concertina*, winner of the 2014 Roanoke Chowan Prize. A new novel, *The Life of the World to Come,* was released in late 2014. His new volume of poems, T*he 13th Sunday after Pentecost*, will be released by LSU Press in 2016. In spring of 2016, Bathanti will serve as the Charles George Veterans Affairs Medical Center Writer-in-Residence. He teaches at Appalachian State University in Boone, NC.

Greg Dawes is a distinguished professor of Latin American Studies and Cultural Theory at North Carolina State University and editor of the peer reviewed electronic journal, *A Contracorriente*. Greg Dawes is from the United States, but spent seven years of his childhood in Argentina and has spent time in several other Latin American countries as well, particularly Chile. His books include *Aesthetics and Revolution: Nicaraguan Poetry*, 1979-1990, *Verses Against the Darkness: Pablo Neruda's Poetry and Politics*, and *Poetas Ante La Modernidad: Las Ideas Esteticas y Politicas de Vallejo, Huidobro, Neruda y Paz*. His next book on Pablo Neruda titled *Multiforme y comprometido: Pablo Neruda después de 1956* will be published in Chile in Fall 2014.

Erdağ Göknar is Associate Professor of Turkish & Middle East Studies at Duke University and an award-winning literary translator. He holds an MFA in Creative Writing from the University of Oregon and a Ph.D. in Middle East Studies from the University of Washington. He has published various articles on Turkish literary culture as well as three novel translations (most recent editions listed): Nobel laureate Orhan Pamuk's *My Name is Red* (Everyman's Library 2010); Atiq Rahimi's *Earth and Ashes* (from Dari, Other Press 2010); and A.H. Tanpınar's *A Mind at Peace* (Archipelago 2011). He is the co-editor of *Mediterranean Passages: Readings from Dido to Derrida* (UNC Press 2008) and the author of the academic study, *Orhan Pamuk, Secularism and Blasphemy: The Politics of the Turkish Novel* (Routledge 2013). His current book project, *Occupied Istanbul: Turkish Subject-Formation from Trauma to Trope*, examines the cultural legacy of the Allied occupation of Istanbul between 1918-23. He leads the Duke in Turkey study abroad program each summer.

Jaki Shelton Green, 2009 Piedmont Laureate, has received a variety of awards and honors for her work, including the North Carolina Award for Literature (2003), Artist-in Residence at The Taller Portobelo Artist Colony (2006) in Panama, and the 2007 Sam Ragan Award. Her poetry has appeared in publications such as *The Crucible, The African-American Review, Obsidian, Poets for Peace, Ms. Magazine, Essence Magazine, KAKALAK, Callaloo, Cave Canem African American Writers Anthology,* and *The Pedestal Magazine.*

Her publications (Carolina Wren Press) include *Dead on Arrival, Dead on Arrival and New Poems, Masks, Conjure Blues, singing a tree into dance, Blue Opal (a play),* and *breath of the song* (which was cited as one of the two Best Poetry Books of the Year by the Independent Weekly).

Terry Randolph Hummer is an American poet, critic, essayist, editor, and professor. His most recent poetry collection is *Ephemeron* (Louisiana State University Press, 2011). He has published poems in literary journals and magazines including *The New Yorker, Harper's, Atlantic Monthly, The Literati Quarterly, Paris Review,* and *Georgia Review.* His honors include a Guggenheim Fellowship inclusion in the 1995 edition of *Best American Poetry,* and two Pushcart Prizes.

Finalists

(In alphabetical order)

॰

Leila Chatti

Spark
      for Mohamed Bouazizi

as a child, they made us fear
cigarette butts and firecrackers

which, when dropped, would catch
everything ablaze. we watched

the flames swallow Californian forests whole,
eying with suspicion the flickering

birthday candle, the onyx cord,
the glistering bulb of the lamp.

when you died, they gave you
two minutes mention on American news

before switching to holiday sales, those red suits
and snowflakes falling like ash.

a December so still I swear I could hear the snap—
match against stone, hiss of life—

and everywhere I looked, fleeting
pinpricks of light, solitary embers burning,

air choked already with smoke.

Leila Chatti

A Woman Walks into Heaven and Hijacks Fate

The eyelids of an Iraqi child blink
open again like a window
shade lifted on a dark night. Dogs
rise from shallow graves,
wag their tails, come inside.
The bullet unburrows itself
like a steel caterpillar worming
its way out of the school wall,
hums through the tunnel of the young
heart, nuzzles back into its gun.
The husband does not leave.
The baby is never lost.
The walls stay standing.
In the marketplace, the parked car
never erupts into light—no plume of fire
a chrysanthemum bloom rising
like its own sun, and all the brilliant
shimmering dust stays whole.
A quiet Sunday.
The man sits back in his seat, turns
the key. Adjusts the mirror and sings
in praise of Her all the way home.

Leila Chatti

Shift

I am far from the man I love.
I marvel a moment
the word: man.
It is new, first
time arrived quietly
on my tongue.
In the beginning,
I said to my mother
I've met a nice boy.
Now, I say I love a good man.
Without my noticing, he walked
from one word's room to another.
My life unfurls as a series of these
small irreversible shifts.
I visit him monthly. Each
time, I look closely,
search his face
for what I've missed.

Leila Chatti

Leila Chatti is a Tunisian-American dual citizen and former special education teacher. She currently resides in Raleigh, North Carolina, where she is a poetry instructor and MFA candidate at North Carolina State University. She was awarded an *Academy of American Poets Prize*, was a 2015 finalist for *the Allison Joseph Poetry Award*, and has published work in *Rattle, decomP*, and elsewhere.

Lois Marie Harrod

Giorgio Morandi

Speak softly, he said, to his colors
and as for the knife?

Only the sort
that gnaws bread.

The fruit has been eaten.
The tipped bowl

remembers
its porridge.

But what else could he paint–
all those broken bottles

falling from the skies
and when the war ceased?

What was left—
a table, a bottle, a little bread?

This much of my life eaten,
still life natura morta—

peaches shrivel
but bottles remain.

It is enough in this world
to have a few things that hold—

Lois Marie Harrod

doesn't the gray
evoke road and snow?

We do not need many notes
to make a song.

Sometimes the flasks seem women
meeting in the piazza.

Sometimes a holy family–
bottle pitcher bowl.

And what are we but vessels?
How can we have done

so much harm?
Let us sit here, quiet.

No shouting.
Like a poet who uses only a few words

candlestick ... bow ...
ink ... pot ... urn.

Isn't it better
than rearranging buildings

Let the table top
become the earth.

Lois Marie Harrod

Vessel

The weaker I am
the less I misunderstand

these chinks, my
meddle and pry,

the places
you've entered

my mouth
my neck.

You have put
your hands

here
and here

and what I take in
you pour out–

which is why
I understand

oil and wine
sand and clay,

what I am
and what I contain.

Lois Marie Harrod

But what
did I know of you

who trusted me
to the Mediterranean

that middle sea
between us.

You sank me
 in tempests

and may
find me yet

glazed and cracked
cork intact.

Lois Marie Harrod

Given These Operations Are Ongoing

If a small femur fell from the sky
and landed on a magnolia leaf
right here, where you can see it
as you descend the steps this morning,
as you leave for your walk, you might
think it was the first drop
of bones the way you sometimes
feel the first drop of rain
and then wait for the next
which usually comes in twos
and threes like children straying
down the sidewalk after the school bus
drops them at the corner,
and then the downpour,
and you are back again
in that terrible gymnasium
where adolescents are screaming
and you have been assigned
crowd control. Who knows
which one will lose his balance
and tumble from the bleachers
or god forbid, though you have
given up belief in protective gods,
the whole section will collapse
and the bodies thunder down,
layers and layers of ribs and teeth,
mammoths, saber-toothed tigers,
a passenger pigeon, sea cow,
one heavy-footed auk–
but this is such a small bone,
the sort you used to pick from

Lois Marie Harrod

owl pellets in eighth grade, and only one,
and now touching it, you can't
remember if it is the femur
of a mouse or a mole or a sparrow,
they are all different
and the chart has blurred
in your mind, you aren't even
sure it is a femur, maybe it is
a small shoulder blade, yes,
let's say it is the shoulder blade
of a black-eyed junco
and there on the leaf beside
it now, the skull of the smallest shrew.

Lois Marie Harrod

Lois Marie Harrod's 13th and 14th poetry collections, *Fragments from the Biography of Nemesis (Cherry Grove Press)* and the chapbook *How Marlene Mae Longs for Truth (Dancing Girl Press)* appeared in 2013. The *Only Is* won *the 2012 Tennessee Chapbook Contest (Poems & Plays)*, and *Brief Term*, a collection of poems about teachers and teaching was published by B*lack Buzzard Press,* 2011. *Cosmogony* won t*he 2010 Hazel Lipa Chapbook (Iowa State)*. She is widely published in literary journals and online ezines from *American Poetry Review* to *Zone 3*. She teaches Creative Writing at The College of New Jersey. Read her work on www.loismarieharrod.org.

Mimi Herman

N-----

Never bigger than a finger
On the trigger, it could
Shoot you in the back.
It could string you up
From a tree that had grown
All those years beside the road.
It said too big for your britches
As if the speaker's itches for power
Hadn't split the seams of discontent.
Wherever that word occurred, violence went.
It was the leader of a mob.
The job of its followers
Was to ensure
You never got
Any bigger.

Mimi Herman

Kike

Neighbors hoarded the word
until, full of empty,
they launched it into the air.
There it floated,
a thing of sticks and string
held together by exquisitely thin skin.

Once aloft, it could not be reeled in.
Its tail trailed the unswept chimneys,
gathering soot and must,
should and dust.

On the tracks below, an engine started,
with creak and grind.
pulling cattle cars
full of never mind.
A storm tore it loose,
The wind picked it up,
dragged it through the battle of myth and kine.

Neighbors herded the word,
until, full of hard,
they thrust it in the pockets
of their Sunday clothes.

They stored it in the stockyards.
They swept it through the streets.
They ground it into the dust that settled
after the ashes rose.

Mimi Herman

Grief

Grief bisects me like a fault line.
Grief sections me like an orange.
Grief dissects me when the fault is mine.
In grief, keep different sections separate,
But synchronize your grief with mine.
Grief infiltrates me like an undercover agent
Everyone's grief becomes mine.
Grief weeps lemon juice and pulp.
Burning the cracked skin.
Grief speaks in the language of lava.
Grief can't afford to be languid
Seek grief before it finds you.
Build fires to burn everything in grief's path.
Who can see past grief?
Grief is luxurious. It spends you.
There is always a tax on grief.
It will clean out your accounts.
It will scrape the numbers off your clock,
And leave the face clean
Dripping with time you might have spent
With the one you're grieving for.

Mimi Herman

Mimi Herman is the author of *Logophilia* and *The Art of Learning*. Her writing has appeared in *Michigan Quarterly Review*, *Shenandoah*, *Crab Orchard Review*, *The Hollins Critic* and other journals. She holds an MFA in Creative Writing from Warren Wilson College. With John Yewell, Mimi offers Writeaways retreats for writers in France and Italy, and on the North Carolina coast. She has been a writer-in-residence at the Hermitage Artist Retreat and the Vermont Studio Center. Since 1990, Mimi has engaged over 25,000 students and teachers in writing workshops. You can find her at www.mimiherman.com and at www.writeaways.com.

Emily Jaeger

BEEKEEPING

you approach from the back,
    servant to a palace.
        Shed your human smell
            between reeds
of lemongrass,
    holding coals in tin jars,
        accordions pumping.
When you slide the knife
    through waxed-over creases,
        you pull off the
wood cover to find
    the moon of a thousand bodies
        humming.
Oxygen of fanned wings
    mountains and gorges of
        hexagonal print wax
            larva capped in
for the winter.
    Honey—smell it
        through the smoke in your
fingers.
    As you sort through the planet
        frame by frame
the workers bump your face
    breasts,
        shoulders,
            convex of kneecap.
Thread your yellow constellation
    for one instant
        onto the morning air.

Emily Jaeger

NOSTALGIA

Sing me one more
yellow song of oblivion:
the neighbor's curse-chant
as he leads the plow.
Drooling oxen
pirouette eight legs
into a single row.

Last year I planted too,
foot-pressed yucca stems
into waterlogged earth.

The *tajy* trees bloom
seven days of yellow,
the last spoonful of winter
cupped in frilly trumpets.

The seeds are underground
and we can still dream
of tubers larger than thighs
before they sprout.

I've returned my field
to the weeds
it's how I say

Emily Jaeger

THE AUTOPSY

*From Female Corpse Back View
Hyman Bloom, 1947*

Oh gentle ones,
grasping your scalpels like lace-makers,
what you would discard
as no heart no brain no lungs:

cumbia squealing down
the column of her spine,
buttocks thick
from sitting Augusts
in the cumin-pepper smell
of her sweat.
Lying alone for years.
Lying with love
and dogs at her feet.

You've drained the blood,
picked the cauliflower-edged
tumor from her uterus
written and left. Now the resting hum.
Now the white room and this week's
cool earth wanting her:
empty hands folded
beneath the chest.

Emily Jaeger

Emily Jaeger is an MFA candidate at UMASS Boston and co-editor/co-founder of Window Cat Press. The recipient of the Mary Curran scholarship for writing, her poetry has appeared or is forthcoming in *Four Way Review, Soundings East,* and *Incessant Pipe Salon* among others. Her chapbook The *Evolution of Parasites* is forthcoming from Sibling Rivalry Press July 2016.

Edison Jennings

Thin Ice

Two feet of snow had buried the fishhooked
reach of sand called Jacob's Nose, and ice sheeted
the brackish Corsica from shore to shore,
bridging snow-bound farms to the snow-stalled town.
Geese and ducks, bundled on the frozen shelf
of river, chorused as I slowly stepped
across the ice; slowly, to be sure—no one
near to hear or help should I, god forbid,
fall in.
       Now I think maybe god forbade,
because the ice was thin and I sit here,
stepping wayward lines, foot by wayward foot,
though waterbirds still fly south in winter,
and snow sometimes still blows across the bay,
and footloose children still sometimes fall in.

Edison Jennings

Trickle Down

Four houses, six cars, three wives, and two kids later,
he despaired: pension, stocks, and bonds, all well balanced,
except for him. So he went to France to despair in style.
Over dinner, a lover asked him how much he was worth.
A lot, he said, maybe more, then went to his room alone,
where he flicked the light, locked the door, thought, not much,
maybe less, and poured himself too many drinks.
Hours passed, the dark grew vast, sweeping Paris in its drift
as he sank to sleep listening to the late-night rain
that rattled on the mansard roofs and slicked the cobbled
Place Vendôme, the runoff sluicing though the gutters,
down the storied sewers, into the streetlight-silvered Seine,
through his lot of nights to follow, into the North Atlantic
beneath the Borealis and a wealth of worthless stars.

Edison Jennings

The Cats of Rome
Bush/Berlusconi Conference, Rome, June 5, 2004

The cats of Rome sleep, feed, and breed
among the tumbled travertine, and slip,
tails high, across the flag draped avenues.
Ignoring pomp, alive to circumstance,
they cruise cafes for crumbs or prowl
the Pantheon.
              Because so many
come and go, for them the coffered cool
is nothing new, and every word is echo.
At the axis of the empire, they curl
round Trajan's column, indifferent
to a fault, at home in a fallen world.

Edison Jennings

Edison Jennings lives in Abingdon, Virginia. His poems have appeared in several journals and anthologies. Jacar Press published his chapbook, *Reckoning*, in 2013.

Anne Whitehouse

CALLIGRAPHIES
Cai Guo-Qiang speaks

In the old days in China
my father collected calligraphy,
ancient scrolls, and rare books.
We lived in Quanzhou,
across the strait from Taiwan.
We could hear artillery batteries
firing into the mist at the island
that still resisted the mainland.

My father's calligraphy
was delicate and adept.
I used to stand at his shoulder,
careful to leave space
for his arm to move freely,
as I watched him wet the ink
to the right consistency,
select his brush, and dip it
gently and carefully, soaking
the soft hairs of the badger,
and stroke its sides
against the jar, forming a point
like no other, soft, flexible, yielding.

With an intake of breath,
he raised his hand that held the brush,
hovering above the paper,
and slowly exhaled
until he was an empty receptacle,
and then, and only then,
he touched the tip of the brush

Anne Whitehouse

to the fine rice paper—
the strokes flowed, deft and sensitive,
forming the ancient shapes of the words.

Then came the Cultural Revolution.
My father worried that his books,
his scrolls, and his calligraphy
were a time bomb ticking.
He buried his collection in a hole
in the earth of the cellar,
but he was still afraid, and little by little,
he began to burn it, at night, in secret,
in the hidden depths of the house.

Afterwards he was not the same.
He lost himself in a strange self-exile
and left us all, his family, behind,
finding perilous refuge
far away in the mountains
in a ruined Buddhist convent,
where an old crone of ninety,
the last remaining resident,
gave him sanctuary.

There he would take sticks
and write calligraphy once more
in puddles on the ground
that would disappear
as soon as it was written,
leaving invisible skeins of sorrow
in the changing reflections
of cloud and sky on water.

Anne Whitehouse

I am his son, and my calligraphy
is fireworks, my art gunpowder,
as evanescent as writing on water.
Pinyin—the Chinese word
means fire medicine, invented
by alchemists investigating immortality.

My explosions are brief dreams,
where space and time combine
in a momentary universe
of birds, fish, and animals,
little-known symbols,
the stream of the Milky Way,
energy transformed into chaos.

In my youth a shaman protected me
from the ghosts of dissatisfaction
that were haunting me,
freeing me to communicate
the invisible within the visible.
Some mysteries are meant to be discovered,
some are meant to remain heaven's secrets.
I imagine an alternate history
where the discovery of nuclear power
was not used for making weapons.
I dream of creating a ladder of fire
far in the air above the earth,
seen from worlds beyond our own.

Anne Whitehouse

BOOKENDS

In memory of my father-in-law, Hugh Lord Whitehouse

I
For days we'd been packing—
the clothes that would fit no one
had been given away,
the rooms were full of boxes
and tagged furniture,
the walls were bare,
closets and cupboards empty.

Yet, stripped of so much,
the house still enchanted us,
enfolded and protected us.
Light through dozens of windows
played over the clean white walls
and stairs and banisters of maple wood.
At the back of the house was the view
over the watery road of the canal
and all the wildlife that lived along it.

The night before the movers came
I made a dinner of triple tail
baked with butter and lemon,
roast potatoes and asparagus,
green salad with tomato,
avocado, and goat cheese—
one last meal to add to
the memorable meals over the years.

Later that night I swam in the pool
in the warm September rain,

Anne Whitehouse

while my husband shot pool
in the next room.
Through the glass doors I glimpsed him
aiming the cue, heard
the clicks of balls being struck.
I dove underwater,
submerged in a sweet,
prolonged farewell.

Dense night, falling rain
on warm water, the air so full
of rain it was like water.

II

Just before everyone left,
I discovered the bookends
interspersed between the books
that no one was taking

and recognized my father-in-law's handiwork
in the blocks of wood four inches square,
each fastened at right angles with two screws
to a square of aluminum.

Made with care, using materials at hand,
the squares of wood sanded and stained,
and the squares of aluminum sanded, too,
so they would slide smoothly
between book and bookshelf.

Presented with the bookends,
my husband dated them from his father's
grad student days, when short on money,

Anne Whitehouse

with mechanical abilities and cultivated tastes,
he made a pair of floor lamps
from salad bowls and ski poles painted black,
with tubular linen shades.

In so much of what he did,
My father-in-law exhibited a painful perfection
that was hard to live up to, hard to live with.
In their serenity and simplicity,
these beautiful objects he made
reveal nothing of his struggles.

Anne Whitehouse

A GIRL WHO FELL IN LOVE WITH AN ISLAND

I thought I saw the ghost of myself
as I was at the age of 27,
standing up on a bicycle, peddling uphill,
long hair streaming behind her.
She smiled as she passed me in the twilight
and wished me a good evening.

On the back of her bike was
a milk crate for hauling things,
the same as I once had.
She was wearing flip-flops
and a loose wrapped skirt.
I had seen her on the beach,
making salutations to the setting sun
over the sea in a reflected fire
of blazing gold and rose embers.
I hadn't wanted to interrupt her,
or show her to herself thirty years older.

I was a girl who fell in love with an island.
Each time I've left here,
something of that quiet, introspective girl
has lingered behind and never left.
On visits when I come across her
she has never gotten any older.

In August I return in search of her,
wearing my oldest clothes, ones she wore,
worn and faded, softened by use.
Once again she and I are one

Anne Whitehouse

when I swim in the cove's cold waters,
gazing up at the sea and sky
or diving underwater to watch
the dark kelps waving over the rocks.

Anne Whitehouse

Anne Whitehouse is the author of five poetry collections—*The Surveyor's Hand, Blessings and Curses, Bear in Mind, One Sunday Morning,* and *The Refrain.* Her novel, *Fall Love*, will be published in Spanish as *Amigos y amantes* in 2015. Born and raised in Birmingham, Alabama, she graduated from Harvard College and Columbia University and lives in New York City.

www.annewhitehouse.com

Andy Young

ON SYRIAN POLITICAL CARTOONIST ALI FARZAT'S
SELF-PORTRAIT, DRAWN IN THE HOSPITAL
  AFTER HIS HANDS WERE BROKEN

his lips drag down his gaze
straight revealing the sneer
that might otherwise be taken
		as the sadness of Damascus
		where he was left
			in a heap on the street

praise the sneer the wilting gaze
he ringed his left eye
with ink to show the bruising
		creased his face and pillow
		with lines jagged as stones'
			filled in the dip of his

own neck the tube in the crook
of his arm praise the exactitude
his hands mummy-wrapped
		broken fingers halved
		by tape and gauze somehow
			he unbent the middle finger

of the right hand made it jut
praise the unbending above
the others away from his body
		in two dimensions it points
		to the heart praise the heart
			maybe the finger really

Andy Young

    didn't unbend maybe it's one
of the fingers which does not
work now this is a self-portrait
        how he sees himself
        how he wants to be seen
                in any case he perched

a pen praise the pen managed
to shade his hair black and gray
his burned beard his posture
        wincing against sheets praise
        the sheets on which he rests
                the sheets on which

he draws himself praise
the ink the printing presses
churning in hidden rooms
        the smudges on hands
        after touching news
                praise food stalls

in occupied squares praise
concrete pilings that smash
down walls praise bandanas
        soaked in vinegar
        praise Fridays
                of chanting

and chanting again knowing
nothing will change anytime
soon praise the cartoons
        of Ali Farzat
        praise Ali Farzat's
                middle finger

Andy Young

Far from Her in Egypt under Curfew
for Iman

We got babysitters
so we could go the Square,
cut lemons for our scarves—
the small, thin triangular ones
she said were for people
of the Book. Wearing one,
you could be any one of the three
religions, she said, though
her Egyptian self is seen
as foreign: her clothes,
her ways, her spot-on
English, and I am always
stared at, an *agnabi*, though
I'm told I have *an Egyptian face*.

Those magnetic paper dolls
on my fridge reminded her
of that video, the headless kid
in Syria, the father holding her
up, looking into where her face
would have been—
can we still speak
of the ishta, its perfumed cream,
its seeds something we could spoon?
Speak of the afternoon light flat
and bright as a copper plate, clatter
of men hawking tomatoes, water,
a stone wheel to sharpen knives,
the voice of that man who could
barely shuffle, his hands out,
his cry catching in his throat
Ya Raab Ya Raab Ya Raab

Andy Young

IN YOU THE REVOLUTION

in you the call to prayer
        in the middle
of the siege in you the banners
                flapping, tent posts
staked in you the smooth face
        as water cannons pelt

you stitch of raw wound
        sight remaining
in the one good eye
                in you intake
of breath against broken rib
        in you blindfold and soldier's

fists quiet in pockets
        in you a kiss
on the cheek of a cop thug
                camel-kindness
stepping over
        uncrushed skull

in you the tank wheels
        stilled by the man
draped cat-like
                across its apparatus
in you the dust undisturbed
        by its tracks

Andy Young

in you the pipe tapped
        to fill up
the jugs in you the bread
               split and split
again in you the salt
        and blanket, the greedy

sleep in you
        the candle lit
under the martyr's face
               smiling from a frame
and lit frames of text
        message going through

tap tapping into metal
        in you
sweet shop and twitter
               peaceful peaceful
on powder feet
        leaving a sugar trail

you ancient and just born
        tea and smoke
as we watch as if through
               a window
a dark screen lit by gun battle
               Molotov cocktails thrown

Andy Young

from rooftops
      and you are
the cooking pot used as a helmet
                the corrugated tin
to shield the blows in you
        the chunk of asphalt

dug from the street
      in you the bandaged
one with crutch
            standing ground
in you that ground
      in you the revolution

February 14th, 2011

Andy Young

Andy Young grew up in West Virginia and teaches at the New Orleans Center for Creative Arts and at Tulane University. Her first full-length collection, *All Night It Is Morning*, was published in November 2014 by Diálogos Books. A graduate of the Warren Wilson Program for Writers, her work has also been published in three chapbooks and in places such as the *Los Angeles Review of Books, Callaloo, Guernica* and the Norton anthology *Language for a New Century*. With her partner, Khaled Hegazzi, she translates Arabic poetry.

Honorable Mentions

(In alphabetical order)

Jane K. Andrews

Visitation

I was not there to see him, I was
on my way through G Wing, past
the nurses' station to the last door on the left.

Straight ahead a steel cart stacked with covered dinner trays
could not contain its odors of fish sticks and collard greens,
and milk that might have soured.

I had to turn aside to go forward and turning
faced a face, dry lips open, blue eyes wide
bulb-shaped head held in place by hands knobbed as crab legs.

Sunk in his seat, staring up at me
he was held fast to his wheelchair
by a velour belt under his skinny arms.

He gurgled at me, a fish out of water,
a drowning man, no rope would save
I smiled as I walked by him.

Like the nurses in the narrow hall
in front of me
I did not look back.

Jane K. Andrews

Obituary

Grief is not original,
it's ubiquitous as sin.
Suffering, let's face it,
is dull.

How to dress it up
so it seems new?
If it were sex,
How-To-Self-Help could say,
Saran Wrap, Redi Whip, take it outdoors,
role play.

But it can't be denied---
an old gift in fresh paper,
a long time lover in period costume,
taken in a national park
is ultimately familiar
as the twenty-third Psalm
at another funeral.

Just as the moves you make
with a new lover
are those you learned from
the one before. The pulse
point on the neck. The stroke
inside a wrist.

Every new grief
opened
reveals, nested inside,
each grief that came before.

Jane K. Andrews

The new contains the old;
each death is every death.

Your grief is a spectacle
and an embarrassment
to others. After eight minutes,
they are bored. And you are bored, too,
your grief blunted,
a professional usher
watching a different production
of the same play. Oh yes. *King Lear.*

It all comes down to skin and bone,
we deny it, but we're wrong.
Our loves and losses mean nothing to anyone
but ourselves. When the lights go out,
we are alone.

Jane K. Andrews

Kern Baby*

Josephine practices blow jobs
on the red and yellow Indian corn
her mother hangs
on the front door
from Columbus Day
until the day after
Thanksgiving.

The ears are old, dry,
and hard---
shucks pulled back, stiff.
No longer green.
The scent of August
long gone.

Josephine knowing
the cobs will soon be replaced
with evergreens,
borrows another year's harvest,
her mouth and tongue running
like water over pebbles
along the column of corn.

Her lips fold against
her teeth,
as if she had the strength to hurt
what has long since
dried.
Josephine closes her eyes
and moans.
her best friend says

Jane K. Andrews

they like that.

Josephine grips
the scratchy husks
with her left hand,
her right slides up and down,
twisting along the slick rows
as she sucks the tip
in and out.

Josephine feels
ready. She has rehearsed
her role until it seems
natural. She is expert at fellating
a vegetable cock she hangs back
on the front door
when she is done.

At fourteen, she is too old
for Trick or Treat, but
she is happy, knowing
November will bring
its Horn of Plenty
and Josephine will be glad
when Thanksgiving comes.
There is so much
to look forward to.

* *A doll or image decorated with corn, grain, flowers, etc,, carried in the festivals of a kem or harvest-home. Also called "Harvest Queen."*

Jane K. Andrews

Jane Andrews has a BA in English from NC State University. Andrews teaches writing and poetry courses through Duke Continuing Education. She is Nonfiction Editor at *The Main Street Rag,* and has earned awards in memoir, personal essay and poetry. Andrews' fiction, essays, memoir and poetry have appeared in *Prime Number Magazine, Red Clay Review, The Dead Mule School of Southern Literature, Verdad Magazine, Kindred, The News and Observer,* and other publications. She is a past board member of *Carolina Wren Press* and *the NC Poetry Society*. Andrews is a freelance writing instructor, workshop facilitator, and book editor.

Mary Elizabeth Parker

Freighted

1.

Night rain spiking the windshield
flares red at the crossing: train

slamming past—silent—whistle cut
by the car heater's roar—train

carries necessaries, carries nothing.
Her friend is driving them, driving,

cornering blackly for hours
through the broad intersecting grid

of this tidal town where the friend
has lived all her life and is now

a strange citizen: widow.
First reports spared

Katrina's worst fallout:
her husband adamantly safe—

now dead, his body criminally
junk in a box.

She riding shotgun did not
know him well, knew only

he savored cigars and fats;
so, craves, for a moment,

Mary Elizabeth Parker

French fries and smoke—
craves to squeeze back from

the next whistle.

2.

Forty years back, 2 a.m. train
a thousand arcs north
of this crossing,

whistled her to orbit—
(girl waiting to be strong
as the yearning yanking her

like trash on a string
to Chicago, then south, south)—
slammed heat, fist

in her flat little gut
when the C & O mooed past, forcing
its seared envelope of shimmer,

where even a girl must hobo—
puppet on a stick bobbing
down the track—escape

from un-breathable morning,
thimble sun oozing
its yellow egg-drop,

Mary Elizabeth Parker

dead-stopped un-breathable noon—
Train just blunt enough, angling
slow between the sandpits

of Campbell Foundry, to sever
the legs of Tommy on the track
(whom she now would not

child-mind again)—escape
from the hot waste:
sand flooding the chutes

in sky so blue it knifed her.

3.

Train a knife now
brightening its blade:
She's failed

her friend at the crossing;
failed those left back who have
died: her mother's fiercely

wounded body, fierce eyes; failed
her granddaughter dancing,
bridal gown flaring,

flapping cygnet of the white—
a tethered-cord disc
in her neck will stop her—

Mary Elizabeth Parker

though her father builds a craft,
lathe-coaxed to a pure Nicomedes curve,
to bear her back and back from the night whistle.

Mary Elizabeth Parker

A Weight of Birds

1.

She wakes to the tingling
of molecules in her thumb-pad

still lightly pressed
to the pearl-gray breast

of an un-nameable bird—feels,
still, the infinitesimally

brittle ribs, the heat of its rapido heart—
revved as if its fuel

is light, sifted—spun-sugar grains—
and now she lumbers up

from her gray body
to thinning light—

her delicacy of attention
at the liminal point where bird dissolves.

2.

Fell dead, an owl perched
on her building's gargoyle—

(woman next apartment
bagged the weight of feathers

Mary Elizabeth Parker

in her freezer, before night coyotes
could drag it to their den

muzzled out in the bayberry hedge
at the municipal library).

Pack thrives,
where one would think

it absolutely could not,
like the marsh-vireo after Chernobyl.

Pet dogs who died this year
from each house in the city

galumph all night with coyotes;
or arrange at the top of stoops

like totems, alert for ceremony.
Her tiny pug caught and killed

the male cardinal and now the nest
she can't find holds its sour

eggs—the spelling
of her watch that won't come:

She whose husband cleaves
to another woman's breaths

sows bread crumbs out from the
closet she waits in—lost

Mary Elizabeth Parker

to him to hear
her bird-heart racing—

breathes her son's chest—
ball of her thumb tracing

the rise of each rib
formed below hers.

3.

Her lover, spied in this city
he has not entered in years,

kept an African gray, loosed
parrot perched big

in the wounded dogwood
at his old front door.

The house condemned
now, yet his love—

aborting the child when they both
feared everything—

waits on the stoop
with a nine-year-old son.

Mary Elizabeth Parker

Jupe Volante

Years gone, villages sunk to
their stones, France bled now
of stunned blue ***milemilemile***
of sky above saturate gold
milemilemile of sunflowers—

even the *jupe volante*
snatched from a Carrefours grocery
(riot-flowered, twirling, flounced,
next to the fruits)—her take-flight skirt—
now flown to

Languedoc, a stolen flicker
of that *pays* where words nearly
but could not
fly. Keening in the brain
today as she spies

a flared, blooming skirt tiered with seed pearls:
Paris, the label says, but the challis's
rent, rubbed raw, another
woman's finished flight;
yet almost

swings
like gypsy dancing bells
and nearly: lifts
her tired limbs and she descries
one blood-red bead

between a pearl and a blue sequin—

Mary Elizabeth Parker

one red drop, to not deign to
best the gods—one, securing
the seamstress
and any girls who pass the skirt on.

Mary Elizabeth Parker is the author of the poetry collection *THE SEX GIRL (Urthona Press)* and 4 chapbooks, including *CAVE-GIRL (Finishing Line Press, 2012)* and *MISS HAVISHAM IN WINTER (FutureCycle Press, 2013)*. She is creator and chair of the *Dana Awards* in the Novel, Short Fiction, and Poetry, now in its 20th year.

Eric M. Saye

"If I forget, O Jerusalem"

When the market crashed
and there were no houses to frame,
my neighbor up the street
started cooking paint thinner and Sudafed
to keep the lights on and feed his kid.

Months later when the police raided,
they found his boy in a bedroom
on a pile of dirty clothes,
and a cop in a hazmat suit,
lugging an assault rifle,
snatched him up by the ankle
and ran for clear air.
From the open trailer door,
he yelled for the paramedics
and held the boy up like a revelatory fish.

My neighbor – handcuffed in the back of a cruiser,
tweaking, singing at the top of his lungs
"Keep on rockin' in the free world" –
might have seen it all:
the cop with his metal staff and plastic robes
looking like an Old Testament prophet
holding one of those Babylonian boys the way you must
before you dash his head against a stone.

Eric M. Saye

The Deacons

Pinned by light,
my back pressed to the west wall of the church,
and the sun slipping behind the pine brake
like a hand along the brow,
I eavesdropped on the deacons –
solitary in the parking lot, the last members
of the congregation to leave that day –
as they shaped music like nothing I'd heard.
They held their Bibles high
the way snakehunters palm mirrors
to angle light down rabbit holes,
their fast rocking ratcheting up the frenzy of their chant.
With my shoulders flush to the sunny wall,
my Huffy abandoned and one apathetic wheel winding down,
I strained for the tenor of that call,
whose every accent was familiar as my name,
yet indecipherable, deadened
like my father calling low from another room.

Eric M. Saye

Proserpina
--after Bernini's *The Rape of Proserpina*

Pluto straps Proserpina across his hip.
The way she rides up his torso,
pushes the brutish perfection of his head,
she is nearly free, but his hot hands
dig into the flawless white of her thigh,
the exquisite pooch of the belly.
If you poured oil down her side, she would
slip free and fall, all her marble skin sprawling
across the Borghese floor. And then what
would she do, this god abducted with the dew
still on her, genius of the cusping, creeping,
peeling open spring?

                In this moment,
she knows her created self is only
another version of the marble tiles,
does not marvel but appalls, sees
even Bernini's flaws in perspective:
her breasts too full, shoulders too strong,
blunt nails, the skin tarnished at the heels.
Her marble, so fragile, will crumble
if she walks, and looking to you, she mewls
like a swarm of flies over an offering.
Once-god, remembering the power of blood
and worship, she creeps out one arm, white
as moonflower, holds the cracking elbow
and shoulder together by will,
and, perhaps beseeching, cups your ankle
like a vice, and turns to you that cheek
with its tear that won't fall.

Eric M. Saye

Mike Saye is a Georgia native. He is completing his third year at Georgia State University's MFA program. He has worked at the literary journal *Five Points* as an editorial assistant, and he currently teaches freshman composition at Georgia State . *His work has been published in Rattle, Town Creek Poetry,* and *Stone, River, Sky: An Anthology of Georgia Poets* (Negative Capability Press, 2015). Contact him via Twitter @Mike_Saye23.

Turkish Poetry Translations

Behçet Necatigil

by Hatice Örün & Jeffrey Kahrs

Behçet Necatigil

Traditions

Frightening me the thought
Lives in a dark basement, imprisoned.
If the lock he's trying to pry open breaks
I know that I'm finished.

I misunderstood that joyful moment
as a form of quiet before
It was butchered into halves
by the howling from his pit.

I didn't lock that thing
downstairs for my pleasure,
but I worked like a dog to keep him there.
That half smile, a fawning look.

Now is not the time. Maybe later.
When he realized he'd been tricked,
The raging sound of being betrayed
Echoed off the walls of his dark place.

Before him many others had stayed
in that darkness, out of sight.
They begged and pleaded—many died.
A few survived and finally saw daylight.

Truth is I'm no executioner: Why
would I want to jail the desire to live?
But if I this was my ambition
Your traditions would beat me to it.

Behçet Necatigil

TO GO OUT

What pulls us to certain books, letters, buildings
is the desire to get out of ourselves.
A turtle walks a path silent
The leaves are fallen, the park dead

Just to sit a little at a place, that's all
And to part after, roads, the world!
As you walk on the streets at night
A young man at a strip joint asks
Shall we go out? Maybe this is love!

One day he sees someone ahead like himself
But it is too late!
Light goes out, the other shore is dark
And so goes around a ball of yarn in a labyrinth

O who is brave like knights
O who is Ferhad, barefoot in the mountains
These times are scarce they wouldn't let us be
O who is love, a doe startled and trapped

Sadly removes the clothes, as the fabric burns
If you have forty, remove all forty, untie!
Removes them if you can handle it, if she did:
A little later starts the fall (season)

World ! Wash your hands in your waters of loneliness.

Behçet Necatigil

Going out

Are you leaving for the streets?
Be careful, trust in God
The street translated means
Losing one half of the self.

Holed up in those rooms
The cool quiet of the house filled you.
You owe all this to its protective walls
That held the waves of friendship
Breaking around you.

Don't go out.
it will ruin this magic
though the house feels so plain.
(Compare your hidden, moldy life
To streets that are fresh and well lit.)

Finally your ruthless soul returns home.
That's exactly how these seductive streets work!
you want to push away any hand
that reaches out to you.
The weather doesn't matter.
You'll return from the street a traitor.
You've seen how they live out there.

Of course it's ridiculous to bring
The wind home because the house
Is too small, but it happens.
And be careful as you leave:
The wind will surely blow
the streets inside.

Behçet Necatigil was born in Istanbul on April 16, 1916. When he was two years old his mother died. After his father married again, he divided his time between the new family and his grandmother. He was valedictorian at Kabataş High School in Istanbul and entered Istanbul University, where he majored in Turkish Language and Literature. After graduating at the top of his class, he taught literature in several high schools, including his alma mater Kabataş, before taking early retirement in 1972. Necatigil's poetry probes the lives of middle class citizens in their home-family-social circle, and he charts their movement from birth to death as they struggle to form an individual identity. In addition to 14 volumes of poetry, he wrote 17 radio plays and translated poetry from German. He catalogued and published *Dictionary of Authors in Turkish Literature* (1960) and a *Dictionary of Major Works in Turkish Literature* (1979). He died of cancer in 1979. After his death, his family established a prize for poetry under his name.

Jeff Kahrs was born in the Hague, Netherlands, and raised in California. He received a B.A. in Dramatic Literature from U.C. Santa Cruz and an M.A. from Boston University, where he studied with Derek Walcott and Leslie Epstein. In 1988 Jeff helped found a reading series in Seattle called *Radio Free Leroy's*, which ran for six years. From 1993 to 2011 he lived in Istanbul, where he taught English in its myriad forms. He co-edited an issue of the *Atlanta Review* on poetry in Turkey, was published in *Subtropics, mediterranean.nu*, and had a chapbook e-published through *Gold Wake Press*. More recently he co-edited a section of the Turkish magazine *Çevirmenin Notu* on English-language poets in Istanbul, and he was published in *Talisman: A Journal Of Contemporary Poetry And Poetics*. He

Hatice Örün was born and raised in Istanbul, Turkey. She completed her undergraduate studies at Boğaziçi University and received her Ph.D from NC State University. After graduation, she started teaching at the same university, where she currently holds the rank of teaching associate professor. Her translations of Mahmoud Darwish's poems were published in *Varlık*, a leading Turkish literary magazine. Her first collection

Artist - Pelin Bali

Pelin Bali has BSc in Computer Science Engineering from Ege University in Turkey. Although she didn't have formal art education, she was always deeply intrested in visual arts, especially painting since childhood. After moving to the US, she devoted more time to her hobby and volunteered to use her creativity for many events organized by the American Turkish Association of North Carolina. She designed all the book covers, the posters, and the logo of Nazim Hikmet Poetry Festival. She also participated in the group exhibition "Sights and Sounds of Istanbul" featuring local artists of Cary, North Carolina.

Made in the USA
Charleston, SC
01 March 2016